MW00478507

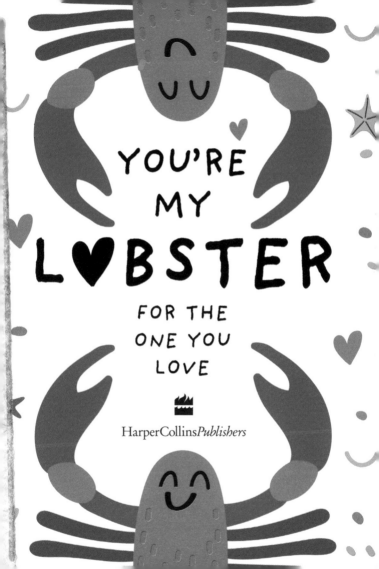

# YOU'RE MY
## LOBSTER

### FOR THE ONE YOU LOVE

HarperCollins*Publishers*

HarperCollins*Publishers*
1 London Bridge Street
London SE1 9GF

www.harpercollins.co.uk

HarperCollins*Publishers*
1st Floor, Watermarque Building, Ringsend Road
Dublin 4, Ireland

First published by HarperCollins*Publishers* 2022

10 9 8 7 6 5 4 3 2 1

© HarperCollins*Publishers* 2022

Pesala Bandara asserts the moral right to be identified as the author of this work.

A catalogue record of this book is available from the British Library.

HB ISBN 978-0-00-850643-8

Printed and bound by PNB, Latvia

All rights reserved. No part of this publication may be reproduced, stored in a retrieval system, or transmitted, in any form or by any means, electronic, mechanical, photocopying, recording or otherwise, without the prior written permission of the publishers.

**MIX**
Paper from
responsible sources
**FSC™ C007454**

This book is produced from independently certified FSC™ paper to ensure responsible forest management.

For more information visit: www.harpercollins.co.uk/green

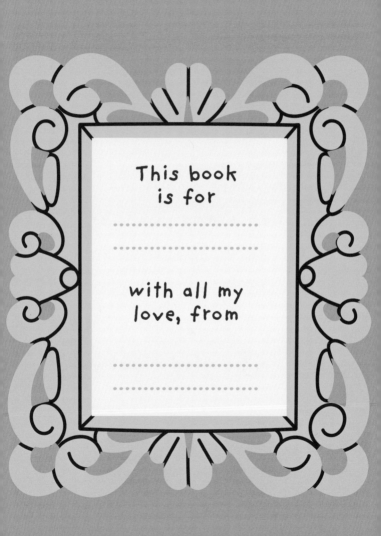

This book
is for

......................................
......................................

with all my
love, from

......................................
......................................

A little about me.
When I was younger,
my dream partner was:

································································

································································

But I'm so glad I got you.

'Someday

my prince

will come ...'

Snow White, Snow White
and the Seven Dwarfs

RACHEL:
Go tell him he's cute. What's the worst thing that could happen?

MONICA:
He could hear me.

*Friends*

# In the story of you and me, who made the first move?

........................................

........................................

## Where?

........................................

........................................

........................................

# Three things I love about you (that no one else would):

1. ............................................
............................................
............................................

2. ............................................
............................................
............................................

3. ............................................
............................................
............................................

'The thing is, um, what
I'm trying to say, very
inarticulately, is that,
um, in fact, perhaps
despite appearances,
I like you, very much.
Just as you are.'

Mark Darcy,
Bridget Jones's Diary

'I burn for you.'

Daphne Bridgerton,

*Bridgerton*

My favourite
nickname for you:

...........................................................

...........................................................

And yours for me:

...........................................................

...........................................................

'Love,
it sustains you.
It's like
oatmeal.'

Captain Raymond Holt,
Brooklyn Nine-Nine

# 'You had me at hello.'

Dorothy Boyd,
Jerry Maguire

# How I remember our first meeting:

· · · · · · · · · · · · · · · · · · · · · · · · · · · · · · · · · · · · · · · · · · · · · · · · · ·

· · · · · · · · · · · · · · · · · · · · · · · · · · · · · · · · · · · · · · · · · · · · · · · · · ·

· · · · · · · · · · · · · · · · · · · · · · · · · · · · · · · · · · · · · · · · · · · · · · · · · ·

· · · · · · · · · · · · · · · · · · · · · · · · · · · · · · · · · · · · · · · · · · · · · · · · · ·

· · · · · · · · · · · · · · · · · · · · · · · · · · · · · · · · · · · · · · · · · · · · · · · · · ·

· · · · · · · · · · · · · · · · · · · · · · · · · · · · · · · · · · · · · · · · · · · · · · · · · ·

· · · · · · · · · · · · · · · · · · · · · · · · · · · · · · · · · · · · · · · · · · · · · · · · · ·

· · · · · · · · · · · · · · · · · · · · · · · · · · · · · · · · · · · · · · · · · · · · · · · · · ·

# 'Our song' is:

....................................................

....................................................

'True love is singing karaoke

"Under Pressure"

and letting the other person sing the Freddie Mercury part.'

Mindy Kaling

# I knew I loved you when...

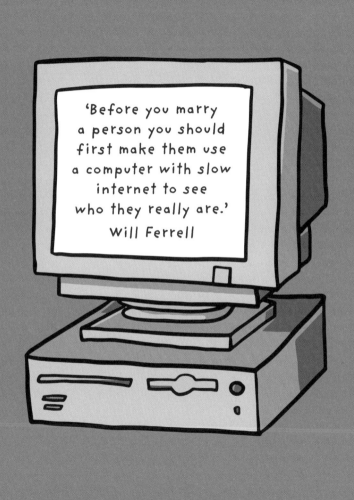

'It would be
a privilege
to have my
heart broken
by you.'

Augustus Waters,
*The Fault in Our Stars*

# The thing I need to work on (even if I don't always like to admit it!):

· · · · · · · · · · · · · · · · · · · · · · · · · · · · · · · · · · ·

· · · · · · · · · · · · · · · · · · · · · · · · · · · · · · · · · · ·

· · · · · · · · · · · · · · · · · · · · · · · · · · · · · · · · · · ·

· · · · · · · · · · · · · · · · · · · · · · · · · · · · · · · · · · ·

· · · · · · · · · · · · · · · · · · · · · · · · · · · · · · · · · · ·

· · · · · · · · · · · · · · · · · · · · · · · · · · · · · · · · · · ·

'So it's not gonna be easy, it's gonna be really hard. And we're gonna have to work at this every day, but I wanna do that because I want you. I want all of you, forever. You and me. Every day.'

Noah Calhoun,
*The Notebook*

# Three places I want to travel to with you:

1. ......................................
......................................
......................................

2. ......................................
......................................
......................................

3. ......................................
......................................
......................................

'You are my
greatest adventure.'

Mr Incredible,
The Incredibles

26

'I'm the squirrel
and you're my nut.
Winter is coming and
I'm gonna store you
in my cheek, girl.'

Schmidt, *New Girl*

'Nothing beats
a first kiss.'

Lucy Whitmore,
50 First Dates

The place where
ours happened:

· · · · · · · · · · · · · · · · · · · · · · · · · · · ·

And it felt:

· · · · · · · · · · · · · · · · · · · · · · · · · · · ·

· · · · · · · · · · · · · · · · · · · · · · · · · · · ·

· · · · · · · · · · · · · · · · · · · · · · · · · · · ·

· · · · · · · · · · · · · · · · · · · · · · · · · · · ·

· · · · · · · · · · · · · · · · · · · · · · · · · ·

'The most exciting, challenging and significant relationship of all is the one you have with yourself. And if you find someone to love the you you love, well, that's just fabulous.'

Carrie Bradshaw,
*Sex and the City*

When we're apart,
I miss:

........................................

........................................

........................................

........................................

And you miss:

........................................

........................................

........................................

........................................

'Marge, I'm going to miss you so much. And it's not just the sex. It's also the food preparation. Your skill with stains of all kind. But mostly, I'll miss how lucky you make me feel each and every morning.'

Homer Simpson,
*The Simpsons*

'I would rather spend
one lifetime with you,
than face all the ages
of this world alone.'

Arwen,
*The Lord of the Rings*

My most cherished
memory of us is:

· · · · · · · · · · · · · · · · · · · · · · · · · · · · · · · · · · · ·

· · · · · · · · · · · · · · · · · · · · · · · · · · · · · · · · · · · ·

· · · · · · · · · · · · · · · · · · · · · · · · · · · · · · · · · · · ·

· · · · · · · · · · · · · · · · · · · · · · · · · · · · · · · · · · · ·

· · · · · · · · · · · · · · · · · · · · · · · · · · · · · · · · · · · ·

· · · · · · · · · · · · · · · · · · · · · · · · · · · · · · · · · · · ·

· · · · · · · · · · · · · · · · · · · · · · · · · · · · · · · · · · · ·

'I hate it when you're not around, and the fact that you didn't call. But mostly I hate the way I don't hate you. Not even close, not even a little bit, not even at all.'

Kat Stratford,
10 Things I Hate
About You

'The dating world is a world of pressure. Let's face it, a date is a job interview that lasts all night. The difference between a date and job interview is: not many interviews is there a chance you'll end up naked at the end.'

Jerry Seinfeld, *Seinfeld*

# My recollections
# of our first date:

. . . . . . . . . . . . . . . . . . . . . . . . . . . . . . . . . . .

. . . . . . . . . . . . . . . . . . . . . . . . . . . . . . . . . . .

. . . . . . . . . . . . . . . . . . . . . . . . . . . . . . . . . . .

. . . . . . . . . . . . . . . . . . . . . . . . . . . . . . . . . . .

. . . . . . . . . . . . . . . . . . . . . . . . . . . . . . . . . . .

. . . . . . . . . . . . . . . . . . . . . . . . . . . . . . . . . . .

. . . . . . . . . . . . . . . . . . . . . . . . . . . . . . . . . . .

The first gift
I gave you was:

· · · · · · · · · · · · · · · · · · · · · · · · · · · · · · · ·

· · · · · · · · · · · · · · · · · · · · · · · · · · · · · · · ·

The first gift
you gave me was:

· · · · · · · · · · · · · · · · · · · · · · · · · · · · · · · ·

· · · · · · · · · · · · · · · · · · · · · · · · · · · · · · · ·

But the best gift you ever
gave me was your heart.

'I've come here with no expectations, only to profess, now that I am at liberty to do so, that my heart is, and always will be, yours.'

Edward Ferrars,
*Sense and Sensibility*

'Lots of people want
to ride with you in
the limo. But you
want someone who
will help you catch
the bus.'

Oprah Winfrey

43

'If you and I had just, well, met ... I would have asked for your number, and I wouldn't have been able to wait twenty-four hours before calling you and saying, "Hey, how about ... oh, how about some coffee or, you know, drinks or dinner or a movie ... for as long as we both shall live?"'

Joe Fox, *You've Got Mail*

Our favourite
TV show to binge-watch
together is:

..........................................

..........................................

..........................................

Our favourite restaurant to
go to on a date
together is:

..........................................

..........................................

..........................................

..........................................

'It's there. I know it is because when I look at you, I can feel it. And I look at you and ... I'm home.'

Dory, *Finding Nemo*

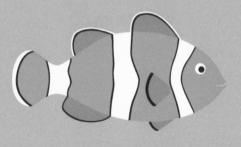

'There's no denying that I have feelings for you that can't be explained in any other way. I briefly considered that I had a brain parasite, but that seems even more far-fetched. The only conclusion was love.'

Sheldon Cooper,
*The Big Bang Theory*

'I came here tonight
because when you
realise you want to
spend the rest of your
life with somebody, you
want the rest of your
life to start as soon
as possible.'

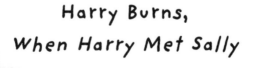

Harry Burns,
*When Harry Met Sally*

# When did we make our relationship official?

................................................

................................................

................................................

................................................

................................................

................................................

................................................

................................................

'She makes the bass drop ... in my heart.'

Jason Mendoza,
*The Good Place*

'It was a great kiss.
If one of us had been
a frog, it would have
had some serious
consequences.'

Lorelai Gilmore,
*Gilmore Girls*

'I'm also just a girl,
standing in front
of a boy, asking him
to love her.'

Anna Scott, *Notting Hill*

# Who said 'I love you' first?

......................................................

# Where?

......................................................

......................................................

......................................................

......................................................

'Love is something sent from heaven to worry the hell out of you.'

Dolly Parton

When did we introduce each other to our family and friends?

........................................

........................................

........................................

And how did it go?

........................................

........................................

........................................

'Obviously, if I was serious about having a relationship with someone long-term, the last people I would introduce him to would be my family.'

Chelsea Handler

'Maybe I do believe it,
all this "meant-to-be"
stuff. Why not believe it,
really? Who doesn't want
more romance in their
life? Maybe it's just up
to us to make it happen.
To show up and be meant
for each other.'

Meredith Grey,
Grey's Anatomy

# The most romantic thing you've ever done for me was:

· · · · · · · · · · · · · · · · · · · · · · · · · · · · · · · · · · · · · · · · · · · · · · · · · · · · · · · ·

· · · · · · · · · · · · · · · · · · · · · · · · · · · · · · · · · · · · · · · · · · · · · · · · · · · · · · · ·

· · · · · · · · · · · · · · · · · · · · · · · · · · · · · · · · · · · · · · · · · · · · · · · · · · · · · · · ·

· · · · · · · · · · · · · · · · · · · · · · · · · · · · · · · · · · · · · · · · · · · · · · · · · · · · · · · ·

· · · · · · · · · · · · · · · · · · · · · · · · · · · · · · · · · · · · · · · · · · · · · · · · · · · · · · · ·

· · · · · · · · · · · · · · · · · · · · · · · · · · · · · · · · · · · · · · · · · · · · · · · · · · · · · · · ·

64

'I guess I kinda hate most things but I never seem to hate you. So I want to spend the rest of my life with you. Is that cool?'

April Ludgate,
*Parks and Recreation*

'Tell you what ... the truth is ... sometimes I miss you so much I can hardly stand it.'

Jack Twist,
Brokeback Mountain

# My favourite thing
# about you is:

......................................

......................................

......................................

......................................

......................................

......................................

......................................

......................................

...........................

My weird habit is:

........................................

........................................

........................................

And your weird habit is:

........................................

........................................

........................................

(I love our weirdness.)

'People are weird.
When we find someone
with weirdness that
is compatible with
ours, we team up
and call it love.'

Dr Seuss

'Some people
are worth
melting for.'

Olaf, Frozen

'Boy, getting off
the freeway makes
you realise how
important love is.'

Cher Horowitz,
*Clueless*

# What is something we've been through together that has made us stronger?

· · · · · · · · · · · · · · · · · · · · · · · · · · · · · · · · · · · · · · ·

· · · · · · · · · · · · · · · · · · · · · · · · · · · · · · · · · · · · · · ·

· · · · · · · · · · · · · · · · · · · · · · · · · · · · · · · · · · · · · · ·

· · · · · · · · · · · · · · · · · · · · · · · · · · · · · · · · · · · · · · ·

· · · · · · · · · · · · · · · · · · · · · · · · · · · · · · · · · · · · · · ·

· · · · · · · · · · · · · · · · · · · · · · · · · · · · · · · · · · · · · · ·

· · · · · · · · · · · · · · · · · · · · · · · · · · · · · · · · · · · · · · ·

· · · · · · · · · · · · · · · · · · · · · · · · · · · · · · · · · · · · · · ·

· · · · · · · · · · · · · · · · · · · · · · · · · · · · · · · · · · · · · · ·

# The most important rule in our relationship is:

........................................

........................................

........................................

........................................

........................................

........................................

........................................

.....................................

'We have a couple of rules in our relationship. The first rule is that I make her feel like she's getting everything. The second rule is that I actually do let her have her way in everything. And, so far, it's working.'

Justin Timberlake

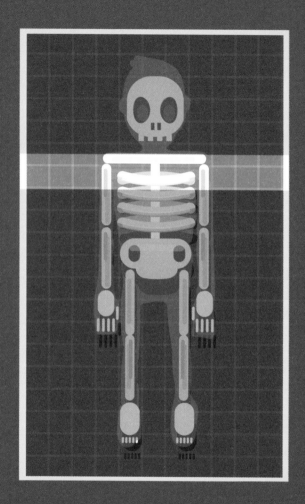

'Love is a lot like backache. It doesn't show on X-rays, but you know it's there.'

George Burns

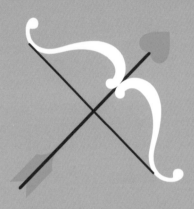

'Endorphins make you
happy. Happy people
just don't shoot their
husbands.'

Elle Woods,
*Legally Blonde*

# Why you make me happy:

........................................................

........................................................

........................................................

........................................................

........................................................

........................................................

........................................................

........................................................

........................................................

'My perfect Valentine's Day? I'm at home, three cell phones in front of me, fielding desperate calls from people who want to buy one of the fifty restaurant reservations I made over six months ago.'

Dwight Schrute, *The Office*

My perfect Valentine's
Day with you would be:

........................................

........................................

........................................

........................................

........................................

82

'I met my soulmate when I was fifteen years old and I have loved her every minute of every day since I first bought her that mint chocolate chip cone. I have loved her through the birth of our children. I have loved her even when I hated her — only married couples will understand that one. And I don't know if it's gonna work out. But I can promise you this, I will never stop trying. Because when you find the one, you never give up.'

Cal Weaver, *Crazy Stupid Love*

'I'm someone who
is looking for love.
Real love. Ridiculous,
inconvenient, consuming,
can't-live-without-each-
other love.'

Carrie Bradshaw,
*Sex and the City*

If I had to describe
our love in three words,
they would be:

1. .....................................................

2. .....................................................

3. .....................................................

'You don't marry someone you can live with, you marry the person you cannot live without.'

Cecelia Ahern,
*P.S. I Love You*

'Penny, we are made of particles that have existed since the moment the universe began. I like to think those atoms travelled 14 billion years through time and space to create us so that we could be together and make each other whole.'

Leonard Hofstadter,
*The Big Bang Theory*

Leela: Don't you ever
wonder about the
future?
Fry: Well, sure, but
you're always in it
... Also, sometimes
Terminators.

*Futurama*

In our future, I see us

........................................

........................................

........................................

........................................

........................................

........................................

together.

'How lucky am I to
have someone that
makes goodbyes
so hard.'

A.A. Milne,
*Winnie-the-Pooh*

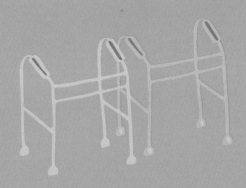

'It's a known fact that lobsters fall in love and mate for life. You can actually see old lobster couples walking around in their tank, you know, holding claws.'

Phoebe Buffay, *Friends*

# You're my lobster because:

· · · · · · · · · · · · · · · · · · · · · · · · · · · · · · · · · · · · · · ·

· · · · · · · · · · · · · · · · · · · · · · · · · · · · · · · · · · · · · · ·

· · · · · · · · · · · · · · · · · · · · · · · · · · · · · · · · · · · · · · ·

· · · · · · · · · · · · · · · · · · · · · · · · · · · · · · · · · · · · · · ·

· · · · · · · · · · · · · · · · · · · · · · · · · · · · · · · · · · · · · · ·

· · · · · · · · · · · · · · · · · · · · · · · · · · · · · · · · · · · · · · ·